The Revolt against Romanticism in American Literature as Evidenced in the Works of S. L. Clemens

The Revolt against Romanticism in American Literature as Evidenced in the Works of S. L. Clemens

By

S. B. LILJEGREN

HASKELL HOUSE PUBLISHERS LTD.
Publishers of Scarce Scholarly Books
NEW YORK, N. Y. 10012
1970

First Published 1945

HASKELL HOUSE PUBLISHERS Lᴛᴅ.
Publishers of Scarce Scholarly Books
280 LAFAYETTE STREET
NEW YORK. N. Y. 10012

Library of Congress Catalog Card Number: 72-146444

Standard Book Number 8383-0583-0

Printed in the United States of America

To

NICHOLAS MURRAY BUTLER

<small>PRESIDENT OF THE AMERICAN ACADEMY OF ARTS AND LETTERS</small>

and

HERSCHEL V. JOHNSON

<small>UNITED STATES MINISTER IN STOCKHOLM</small>

These Essays and Studies

Are Gratefully Dedicated

CONTENTS

CONTENTS

The Revolt against Romanticism in American Literature as Evidenced in the Works of S. L. Clemens.*

In his masterly short survey of *American Literature*, published in 1933,[1]) Carl van Doren says that "American literature is the only important literature in the world which is younger than the art of printing."[2]) This is, of course, an exaggeration. American writers with a world-wide reputation like Emerson, Longfellow, and Whitman were actually conditioned by Old English and Middle English literature no less than were Shakespeare and Milton. American culture is no doubt a part of English culture transplanted to a new continent and there subjected to a separate development. The challenging form which Van Doren has given to his statement, may partly be due to that species of American nationalism which objects to the contention that the United States are still an English colony, intellectually, long after the political Declaration of Independence.[3])

But there is no denying that the English attitude of indifference towards the nascent literature beyond the Atlantic has likewise influenced American development in this respect.

The effort to assert their intellectual independence noticeable on the part of American writers is stimulated by the fact that

---

* The present study on American Romanticism forms part of a series of investigations into that subject pursued for more than twenty years. During that period, access to American libraries was had for a year only. This is somewhat of a drawback, and I cannot hope that nothing relative to my subject has escaped my attention. My consultation in European libraries of more than four hundred volumes of American philological reviews and of as many English, French, and German ones should, however, imply a certain guarantee that the most important and novel finds documented in the present study (the American attack on the terror novel, the terror ballad, the Romantic elegy, the Romantic historical novel, etc.) are chiefly my own. Such is also the case with still more startling discoveries, such as Cooper's debt to *Ossian* and *Werther*. I may add that much of the material gleaned from the reviews, but not incorporated with this study, will be used in future portions of my investigations into American Romanticism.

there is an obvious unwillingness in English intellectual circles to accept both the intrinsic and the relative value of American culture. Authors like Washington Irving, Poe, Cooper, or Longfellow were always popular in England,[4]) but there is a marked reluctance on the part of their English readers to set *Rip Van Winkle*, *The Masque of the Red Death*, *The Deerslayer* or *Evangeline* side by side with English letters. Only very late did Compton Rickett, for example, include a chapter on American literature in his deservedly popular *History of English Literature,* but a corresponding section is still missing in other similar handbooks.[5])

In the same way, a scholarly study of American literature is scarcely pursued in English universities. There is the instance of Henry James. He had a special claim to the interest of English scholars, seeing that he not only deserted his mother-country and settled in England, but even gave up his American citizenship in order to acquire an English one. Even so, of some four or five investigations known to me which have been devoted to Henry James since his death, none is English; one is Swedish, two American, a fourth French, and a fifth German.[6])

The situation is adequately characterized by an authoritative English scholar who says on this subject:

"Twenty years ago a British-American Committee, looking round for some material to mark the approaching completion, in the year 1914, of one hundred years of peace among the English-speaking peoples, made what seemed to them the surprising discovery that there existed in this country no stated teaching of American History; that in no British University, or any other institution of learning and enlightenment in this island, was any Chair, Lectureship, or other rostrum to be found for the dissemination of truth about the History, Literature, and Institutions of certainly the most numerous, and in some respects most powerful and impressive portion of the English-speaking world." [7])

The fact that, after the conclusion of the first World War, a chair of American History was instituted in an English University, had no immediate consequences for the study of American literature in England.[8])

Accordingly, the United States simply *had* to take matters into their own hands, to institute chairs of American literature in American universities and to write the history of their own literature. No wonder, then, that overmuch stress has been put on the intellectual independence of the United States and that the opinion is prevalent among scholars that American literature begins with Franklin and not with Beowulf.[9]

Here, I think, we must look for part explanation of the fact that the actual interdependence of the literary tradition on both sides of the Atlantic has been either frankly denied or, at best, minimized. Among the five chapters in the above-mentioned survey of Van Doren's (Colonial, National, Continental, Imperial, Critical), there is not a single headline which reminds the reader of the terminology of English or European histories of literature, just as if this terminology did not apply to the United States.[10] If we scan the pages of the book, its contents actually bear out the statement in the previous sentence. The work of Washington Irving or Cooper, of Howells or Dreiser is now and then termed romantic or realistic to suit the case. But there is nothing to indicate that Irving and Cooper[11] belonged to the international brotherhood of Romanticists, Howells and Dreiser to that of literary Realists. That is to say: American literature, according to Van Doren, has learnt practically nothing from abroad. That is what it amounts to.

The picture is not much different if we turn to other similar handbooks. Compton Rickett has a heading *Transcendentalism*, it is true, but otherwise scanty or no hints of the interdependence of American and European, particularly English, Romanticism.[12] Under the heading *The Classical Period,* Fischer lists American Romanticists, and some others. Only occasionally does he point out Romantic elements in American letters and their European (English) origin.[13] Surely, this is not satisfactory.

It is not my intention here to trace the history of English Romanticism in the United States. This will be the task of other investigations now preparing. Moreover, the fact is obvious and needs no postulate. What we are trying to do here, is of a different nature.

We all know that in Europe, Romanticism, like most other similar group movements, called forth a reaction. This reaction is called Victorianism, or Realism, in English letters. We are not here concerned with the adequateness of this terminology or with the demarcation of the frontiers of Romanticism and Realism. What we should like to draw attention to, is the fact that, according to the general conception of the history of American literature, there is no such reaction across the Atlantic.

As far as Transcendentalism is concerned, this opinion may to a certain extent be true;[14]) because Transcendentalism was never challenged as English Romanticism was in the eighteen-thirties. If the so-called *Post-Mortem* period has been exposed to some trenchant criticism or even obloquy, this was not due to the fact that the critics traced Transcendentalism in Aldrich.

We must here make a certain distinction which has not so far been made, at least not distinctly enough. There is the recognized form of Romanticism in the United States called Transcendentalism. But this sort of Romanticism was not essentially a literary movement. It was in the main what Romanticism seemed to be to the young Coleridge and the young Southey: a new form of life.[15]) Broadly speaking, American Transcendentalism might be reduced to a maxim: "plain living and high thinking," which hailed from Rousseau, *ultimately*, and which meant more to its adherents than mere new forms of literary expression. Thus, the most obvious manifestation of Transcendentalism was not a novel, a collection of lyrics, or a drama, but an attempt at a new community, or way of living, which we witness first in the Brook Farm Experiment and then in other experiments like Fruitlands and Thoreau's period at Walden Pond. That Transcendentalism was not, in the main, poetry, but philosophy, is further shown by the fact that the name was derived from Kant via Coleridge, and pointed beyond the material world.[16])

Parallel with this Romanticism of a, so to speak, spiritually utilitarian kind, we have Romanticism proper, whose features are well known from European literature. This aspect of the matter has been disregarded on account of the rapt attention which has focussed upon the eccentric enterprise at Brook Farm.

The second kind of American Romanticism has been, in part, something different from Transcendentalism, in part, fused with it — as in the case of Hawthorne. Authors like Charles Brockden Brown, Cooper, and Poe do not require to be associated with the Transcendentalists, as has sometimes been done in order to straighten things out in literary history. Cooper never left us in doubt about his place in literature.[17]) He openly proclaimed that he wanted to do for his mother country what Walter Scott had done for England: write its history in the form of the historical novel. It is necessary to keep this in mind.

In this way, we must be prepared for something approaching European Romanticism in American literature. In addition, as English literature was also the inheritance of the United States, Scott, Coleridge, Wordsworth, Byron, and other English poets likewise formed part of intellectual life across the Atlantic. And so American poets and American readers had to take a definite stand as regards the most obvious manifestations of Romanticism: the historical novel, the terror novel, the terror ballad, the "magnanimous incident" ballad,[18]) the wistful churchyard elegy, the Middle Age pageantry, the nature worship, and so on. In fine, American poets and American readers had to show their colours as to all these things, either accepting or rejecting them. Acceptance meant Washington Irving, Cooper, Poe, Hawthorne, Longfellow, and others, and their readers. But what followed from rejection?

This leads us back to the question put previously in this essay: was there ever a definite reaction against Romanticism in the United States? I know of no historian of American literature who has even been aware of the question.[19]) We hear of Howells as the first real representative of Realism, but where is his attack on Romanticism? Where are the parodies, the satire, the ridicule poured on Romanticism as we know them from the works of Thackeray?

It seems to me that we should re-estimate, from this point of view, the work of some of the leading authors who have shaped the evolution of American letters.

We shall here insert the categorical assertion that, in our opinion, both American and European criticism generally labours under a pronounced misconception as to the quality and place in the world of literature of Samuel Langhorne Clemens, *alias* Mark Twain. In Europe, he is popularly believed to be a sort of literary clown whose witticism appeals to essentially un-educated circles. Even in the United States, he is regarded either superciliously or admiringly as an "enfant terrible" of literature, something in the line of his own Tom Sawyer. His work is considered to be either futile from a literary point of view, or absolutely original, in both cases owing to the fact that, as it is thought, he was part a "Wild West" cowboy, part a prac-tically unlettered visionary of busy young America of the im-mense future. His readings are as desultory as his education, they say, and very narrow, not at all literary. He is a practical man rooted in the busy workaday world, and no poet who has pored over poets. He is the real anti-traditionalist and ico-noclast, irreverent and scoffing at other people's sacred ideals. And so on [20])

This is not satisfactory, in my opinion. Mark Twain is well read in English and American literature.[21]) To some extent, his interest went beyond that. He is not only a cultured man but a man of a refined mind. He has an inborn reverence for tra-dition and the past of mankind. He is only in some measure that prophet of young iconoclast America who holds the stage in the eyes of his admirers as well as of his critics. Anyone who reads his *Innocents Abroad* will remember the overwhelming impression made upon him by the past of Palestine and of Egypt. The Cheops pyramid simply takes his breath away, so that, afterwards, it makes him ashamed of himself to have been impressed to such a degree. And so he has to cut some capers to show the spectators that he is his old irrepressible self. Even Sherman has noticed the clash between "All who know what pathos there is in memories of days that are accomplished and faces that have vanished," and the Egyptian engine driver's impatient words when he is feeding his locomotive with mum-mies: "Damn these plebeians, they don't burn worth a cent — pass out a king." This is not the literary regisseur, as Sher-man thinks, but the cultured mind which does not forget what is expected from him as a witty writer, even in his serious moods.[22])

As a matter of fact, Mark Twain has shown evidence of possessing a detailed knowledge of parts of German literature, and of English and American Romanticists, in particular Walter Scott and Cooper. And it is possible to prove that his knowledge was no less intimate as regards some writers whom he mentions only in passing, or even not at all.

The refinement of mind appearing in the one amongst his books which he liked best of all — *Joan of Arc* — and in many places in his travel books, is no eccentricity — how could it be? — as his critics seem to imply. On the contrary, that sad, wistful face which increasingly awed some of his admirers towards the end of his life, is more the expression of the substance of the man than his jolly short stories or his rollicking lectures. Mental refinement cannot be adopted for an hour without being shown up, but the whimsical face can be the mask of a life-time.

There is a close connection between this fact and Mark Twain's position in the literary tradition not only of the United States but of Europe, and in particular of England. He is no literary buffoon to scoff at ideas or conceptions he does not understand because he has not mastered them, or because he has only a *prima facie* knowledge of them. He both read, grasped, and had clear conceptions and aims as regards literature, as well as any of the literary men of his time on both sides of the Atlantic. As Romanticism pervaded the atmosphere round him in his youth — the middle of the 19th century — he began as a Romantic *at heart* and actually retained a "penchant" for Romanticism all his life.[23]) But at an early period, in the beginning of the sixties, he met men like Artemus Ward and Bret Harte, who were in the same position but who had scented new currents in literature, Realism. Thus Mark Twain became one of them and, with his usual wholeheartedness, went in for the reaction against literary Romanticism more violently than any of his companions.

The most interesting information we have about Mark Twain's early literary predilections and activity is contained in the autobiographical section of *The Innocents at Home*. From Chapter VI of this book, we can extract several details which confirm the view of the early Mark Twain offered above. With his brother Orion he arrived in Nevada in 1661, and in the beginning of the following year accepted a position on the *Virginia City Enterprise*. His own account of his engagement on the *Weekly Occidental* seems to me to hint that at the time he was still a Romantic as far as literature was concerned.[24]

A preliminary note will here explain the nature of Mark Twain's first prose adventure.

The most notable feature of Romanticism in the eyes of the general public was undoubtedly the terror element as manifested in the novel. The first terror novel of importance for the *genre* appears to be Horace Walpole's *The Castle of Otranto*, published in 1764. Walpole achieved a great success with his little sketch of a hundred pages. It became the source of the novels of Clara Reeve, Ann Radcliffe, Matthew Lewis, and others.

The pure terror novel chiefly attracted second-rate writers, and so it came about that it remained primitive both in structure and invention. The characters, plots, events, and tricks of each successive terror novel were taken over more or less mechanically from previous works of the *genre*. The characters preferred were, socially: princes or princesses (Manfred in *The Castle of Otranto*), dukes or duchesses, earls, counts, barons, etc.; morally, they were satanic wily scoundrels (often foreigners, preferably Italians: Manfred in *The Castle of Otranto*, Schedoni in *The Italian*), low blood-thirsty blackguards and ruffians (*The Romance of the Forest*), sorcerers and alchemists in league with the devil (Ambrosio in *The Monk*, Vathek in Beckford's novel). The plots were all mystery and crime, with a preference for family secrets which were usually revealed in the last chapter (as is well known, the terror novel is the father of the detective story); the staple of the plot of course includes murder in its most hideous form, supernatural incidents with ghosts, devils, angels, and the like, conjuration and incantation scenes, black magic, blasphemy, crimes against religion, general evil-doing, etc. The tricks chosen to throw these events into relief are night, darkness, and thunderstorms, the mysterious creaking of doors or ghostly knocking thereon, trap-doors, or the opening of the earth under the feet of the evil-doer, strawberry-marks to reveal the mysteries of relationship (Theodore in *The Castle of Otranto*).

The heroines are the incarnation of beauty, even if they are evil (the beautiful blonde Mathilda in *The Monk*). Intended or achieved incest is common (Walpole's *The Mysterious Mother*). Attempts at suicide occur, which sometimes permit the dead to return to earth, whether in the flesh or as ghosts. And so on.[25])

To return to Mark Twain's account of his early work on the *Weekly Occidental*.

Both the novel pieced together by collaborators, of which he was engaged to write a chapter, and the ballad which he says he actually wrote for the review, were evidently in the vein of the terror novel and of the terror ballad. But the spirit may have suffered a change. When he noted down the narrative of his literary beginnings, he had turned from Romanticism, and so both passages became fierce attacks on the Romantic school. We shall hear his own words.

Mark Twain begins by telling us about the attempt at writing a novel by collaboration made under the auspices of the Review. Several of the staff including himself undertook to write a serial which was intended to appeal to the taste of the public. A woman novelist made a start and introduced a Romantic heroine whose life grew more and more involved thanks to the following collaborators, one of whom got drunk and practically killed all the characters except the Devil. The way in which all this is described, puts ridicule on such elements of the terror novel as were cherished by Walpole, Ann Radcliffe, and Matthew Lewis: the heavenly beauty of the heroine, the exalted social station of the hero, the criminal element, the supernaturalism and the Devil, the secrets, mysteries, strawberry-marks, etc.:

"We expected great things of the *Occidental*. Of course it would not get along without an original novel, and so we made arrangements to hurl into the work the full strength of the company. Mrs. F. was an able romancist, of the ineffable school whose heroes are all dainty and all perfect. She wrote the opening chapter, and introduced a lovely blonde simpleton who

talked nothing but pearls and poetry, and who was virtuous to
the verge of eccentricity. She also introduced a young French
Duke of aggravated refinement, in love with the blonde. Mr. F.
followed next week, with a brilliant lawyer, who set about get-
ing the Duke's estates into trouble, and a sparkling young lady
of high society, who fell to fascinating the Duke and impairing
the appetite of the blonde. Mr. D., a dark bloody editor of
one of the dailies, followed Mr. F., the third week, introducing
a mysterious Rosicrucian, who transmuted metals, held consulta-
tions with the devil in a cave at dead night, and cast the horo-
scope of the several heroes and heroines in such a way as to
provide plenty of trouble for their future careers, and breed a
solemn and awful public interest in the novel. He also introduced a cloaked and masked melodramatic miscreant, put him
on a salary, and set him on the midnight track of the Duke,
with a poisoned dagger. He also created an Irish coachman,
with a rich brogue, and placed him in the service of the society-
young-lady with an ulterior mission to carry billet-doux to the
Duke.

About this time there arrived in Virginia a dissolute stranger,
with a literary turn of mind — rather seedy he was, but very
quiet and unassuming, and kindly, whether he was sober or
intoxicated, that he made friends of all who came in contact
with him. He applied for literary work, offered conclusive evidence that he wielded an easy and practised pen, and so Mr.
F. engaged him at once to help write the novel. His chapter
was to follow Mr. D.'s and mine was to come next. Now what
does this fellow do but go off and get drunk, and then proceed
to his quarters and set to work, with his imagination in a state
of chaos, and that chaos in a condition of extravagant activity.
The result may be guessed. He scanned the chapters of his
predecessors, found plenty of heroes and heroines already
created, and was satisfied with them; he decided to introduce
no more; with all the confidence that whisky inspires, and all
the easy complacency it gives to its servant, he then launched
himself lovingly into his work; he married the coachman to the
society-young-lady, for the sake of the scandal; married the Duke
to the blonde's stepmother, for the sake of the sensation; stopped

the desperado's salary; created a misunderstanding between the devil and the Rosicrucian; threw the Duke's property into the wicked lawyer's hands; made the lawyer's upbraiding conscience drive him to drink, thence to delirium tremens, thence to suicide; broke the coachman's neck; let his widow succumb to contumely, neglect, poverty, and consumption; caused the blonde to drown herself, leaving her clothes on the bank with the customary note pinned to them, forgiving the Duke, and hoping he would be happy; revealed to the Duke, by means of the usual strawberry mark on left arm, that he had married his own long·lost mother and destroyed his long-lost sister; instituted the proper and necessary suicide of the Duke and the Duchess in order to compass poetical justice; opened the earth and let the Rosicrucian through, accompanied with the accustomed smoke and thunder and smell of brimstone, and finished with the promise that in the next chapter, after holding a general inquest, he would take up the surviving character of the novel and tell what became of the devil."[26])

Mark Twain follows up this attack yet more vigorously, relating how the staff protested against this terror novel drivel and were promised redress by the unfortunate author. However, when settling down to work once more, the latter got drunk again and produced a yet more farcical travesty of the terror novel. Mark Twain veiled the whole under an account of how the review went smash immediately after, so that control of his narrative became impossible.

When Mark Twain attacked Romanticism it did not suffice for his satirical purpose to explode the terror novel and leave the other literary genres represented in Romanticism unmolested. And so he added a section, in this very chapter, intended to demolish more Romantic literature and more Romantic authors. This time, it was Romantic poetry at which he drew his bow.

Here, we must recall the following facts.

It is well known that terror ballads played a conspicuous part in the history of the Romantic Movement. Without here entering upon an analysis of the significance of Percy's *Reliques* in this respect,[27]) we should like to state that Bürger's *Lenore* was a

constant source of inspiration to the English Romantic poets,
and that it was repeatedly translated, from Scott onwards,[28]
amongst others by Rossetti. Its sway in English Romanticism
was undisputed until the appearance of Coleridge's *Ancient
Mariner*. Originated in a dream, the latter ballad introduced
the change of scene necessary for it to become popular in England. The churchyard was exchanged for the sea, the original
terror element remaining constant. This *motif* of the sea was
not invented by Coleridge, but only adopted from an old tradition including ballads like *Sir Patrick Spens*. Further, Coleridge abandoned the measure of *Lenore* in favour of the most
popular English ballad measure, known from *The Chevy Chase,
Sir Patrick Spens, Sir Hugh of Lincoln, The Bailiff's Daughter of
Islington, John Gilpin*, Goldsmith's and Chatterton's ballads, etc.[29]

The glimpses of seascape in *The Ancient Mariner*, though
conventional enough to modern readers, stuck in the minds of
Coleridge's contemporaries and followers:

> "And now the storm-blast came, and he
> Was tyrannous and strong:
> He struck with his o'ertaking wings,
> And chased us south along.
> With sloping mast and dipping prow,
>
> . . . . .
> The ship drove fast, loud roared the blast,
> And southward aye we fled.
> And now there came both mist and snow,
> And it grew wondrous cold:
> And ice, mast-high, came floating by,
> As green as emerald.
>
> . . . . .
> The fair wind blew, the white foam flew,
> The furrow streamed off free:
>
> . . . . .
> The stars were dim, and thick the night,
> The steerman's face by the lamp gleamed white;"

There has never been any doubt as to the powerful and
widespread influence of Coleridge's *Ancient Mariner*.[30] It has

been traced in poets and poems as unlike Coleridge and his
ballad as possible. Even *Peter Bell* (cf. *inf.*) has expressions
reminding the reader of the ballad in question. For our purpose
we shall restrict ourselves to a single case, that of Longfellow's
Wreck of the Hesperus.

The content of this ballad is as follows:

The skipper of the schooner Hesperus has taken his little
daughter with him on a winter voyage. He disregards the
warnings of an old sailor, who predicts a hurricane in terms
reminding us of the *Ancient Mariner:* "Last night the moon
had a golden ring, and tonight no moon we see." But the
hurricane sets in, the skipper tries to console his little daughter
who hears signs of death and distress in the night, and finally
he ties her to the mast for security. Ice covers the schooner flying
before the storm, and in the morning, a fisherman sees the little
girl tied to the mast of the shipwrecked boat:

"It was the schooner *Hesperus,*
That sailed the wintry sea;
And the skipper had taken his little daughter,
To bear him company.

Blue were her eyes as the fairy-flax,
Her cheeks like the dawn of day,
And her bosom white as the hawthorn buds,
That ope in the month of May.

The skipper he stood beside the helm,
His pipe was in his mouth,
And he watched how the veering flaw did blow
The smoke now West, now South.

Then up and spake an old Sailor,
Had sailed the Spanish Main,
'I pray thee, put into yonder port,
For I fear a hurricane.

Last night the moon had a golden ring,
And tonight no moon we see.'
The skipper he blew a whiff from his pipe,
And a scornful laugh laughed he.

Colder and louder blew the wind,
A gale from the North-east,
The snow fell hissing in the brine,
And the billows frothed like yeast.

Down came the storm, and smote amain
The vessel in its strength,
She shuddered and paused, like a frighted steed,
Then leaped her cable's length.

'Come hither, come hither, my little daughter,
And do not tremble so.
For I can weather the roughest gale
That ever wind did blow.'

He wrapped her warm in his seaman's coat,
Against the stinging blast:
He cut a rope from a broken spar,
And bound her to the mast.

'O father, I hear the church-bells ring,
O say, what it may be?'
'Tis the fog-bell on a rock-bound coast,'
And he steered for the open sea.

'O father I hear the sound of guns,
O say, what may it be?'
'Some ship in distress, that cannot live
In such an angry sea.'

'O father, I see a gleaming light,
O say, what may it be?'
But the father never answered a word,
A frozen corpse was he.

Lashed to the helm, all stiff and stark,
With his face turned to the skies,
The lantern gleamed through the gleaming snow
On his fixed and glassy eyes.

Then the maiden clasped her hands and prayed
That saved she might be:
And she thought of Christ, who stilled the waves,
On the lake of Galilee.

And fast through the midnight dark and drear,
Through the whistling sleet and snow,
Like a sheeted ghost the vessel swept
Towards the reef of Norman's Woe.

And ever the fitful gusts between
A sound came from the land:
It was the sound of the trampling surf,
On the rocks and the hard sea-sand.

The breakers were right beneath her bows,
She drifted a dreary wreck,
And the whooping billow swept the crew
Like icicles from her deck.

She struck where the white and fleecy waves
Looked soft as carded wool,
But the cruel rocks, they gored her side
Like the horns of an angry bull.

Her rattling shrouds, all sheathed in ice,
With the masts went by the board:
Like a vessel of glass, she stove and sank,
Ho, ho, the breakers roared.

At daybreak, on a bleak sea-beach,
A fisherman stood aghast,
To see the form of a maiden fair
Lashed close to a drifting mast.

The salt sea was frozen on her breast,
The salt tears in her eyes:
And he saw her hair, like the brown sea-weed,
On the billows fall and rise.

> Such was the wreck of the *Hesperus*,
> In the midnight and the snow:
> Christ save us all from a death like this,
> On the reef of Norman's Woe."[31])

It is worth noticing that Longfellow has kept the measure of Coleridge's ballad.

The sentimental or even lachrymose note of Longfellow's poem seemed calculated to evoke the immediate retort of a parodist. In any case, there can be little doubt that Mark Twain saw an opportunity of hitting out at the tradition of *The Ancient Mariner* via *The Wreck of the Hesperus*.[32])

When he wrote his *Aged Pilot Man*, Mark Twain retained the measure of the early ballad models with some variations as also used by Coleridge. The title of the poem aped that of *The Ancient Mariner* both in its syllabification and its rhythm. Mark Twain's *aged* strikes the note of a parody from the beginning. The scene is whittled down to a canal, where a boat is being towed by two mules on shore. We have all the paraphernalia of storm and rain and impending ship-wreck. A dauntless hero, the pilot stands towering above the crew and says over and over again: "Fear not but trust in Dollinger and he will fetch you through." A fling at Lord Byron is made particularly obtrusive; his works are thrown overboard to lighten the ship:

"The Aged Pilot Man.

> On the Erie Canal it was,
> All on a summer's day,
> I sailed forth with my parents
> Far away to Albany.
>
> From out the clouds at noon that day
> There came a dreadful storm,
> That piled the billows high about,
> And filled us with alarm.
>
> A man came rushing from a house,
> Saying, "Snub up your boat I pray!

Snub up your boat, snub up, alas!
Snub up while yet you may."

Our captain cast one glance astern,
Then forward glanced he,
And said, "My wife and little ones
I never more shall see."

Said Dollinger the pilot man,
In noble words, but few, —
"Fear not, but lean on Dollinger,
And he will fetch you through."

The boat drove on, the frightened mules
Tore through the rain and wind,
And bravely still, in danger's post,
The whip-boy strode behind.

"Come 'board, come 'board, the captain cried,
Nor tempt so wild a storm;"
But still the raging mules advanced,
And still the boy strode on.

Then said the captain to us all,
"Alas, 'tis plain to me,
The greater danger is not there,
But here upon the sea.

So let us strive, while life remains,
To save all souls on board,
And then if die at last we must,
Let . . . I cannot speak the word!"

Said Dollinger the pilot man,
Tow'ring above the crew:
"Fear not, but trust in Dollinger,
And he will fetch you through."

"Low bridge! low bridge!" all heads went down,
The labouring bark sped on;
A mill we passed, we passed a church,
Hamlets and fields of corn;

And all the world came out to see,
And chased along the shore,

Crying, "Alas, Alas, the sheeted rain,
The wind, the tempest's roar!
Alas, the gallant ship and crew,
Can *nothing* help them more!"

And from our deck sad eyes looked out
Across the stormy scene;
The tossing wake of billows aft,
The bending forests green,

The chickens sheltered under carts,
In lee of barn the cows;
The skurrying swine with straw in mouth,
The wild spray from our bows!

"She balances!
She wavers!
Now let her go about!
If she misses stays and broaches to,
We're all" — (then with a shout),
"Huray! huray!
Avast! belay!
Take in more sail!
Lord, what a gale!
Ho, boy, haul taut on the hind mule's tail."

"Ho! lighten ship? ho! man the pump!
Ho, hostler, heave the lead!"
"A quarter-three! — 'tis shoaling fast!
Three feet scant!" I cried in fright,
"Oh, is there no retreat?"

Said Dollinger the pilot man,
As on the vessel flew,
"Fear not, but trust in Dollinger,
And he will fetch you through."

A panic struck the bravest hearts,
The boldest cheek turned pale;
For plain to all, this shoaling said
A leak had burst the ditch's bed!
And, straight as bolt from crossbow sped,
Our ship went on, with shoaling lead,
Before the fearful gale!

"Sever the tow-line! Cripple the mules!"
Too late! . . . . . There comes a shock!
Another length, and the fated craft
Would have swum in the saving lock!

Then gathered together the shipwrecked crew
And took one last embrace,
While sorrowful tears from despairing eyes
Ran down each hopeless face;
And some did think of their little ones
Whom they never more might see,
And others of waiting wives at home,
And mothers that grieved would be.

But of all the children of misery there
On that poor sinking frame,
But one spoke words of hope and faith,
And I worshipped as they came:
Said Dollinger the pilot man —
(O brave heart, strong and true) —
"Fear not but trust in Dollinger,
For he will fetch you through."

Lo! scarce the words have passed his lips
The dauntless prophet say'th,
When every soul about him seeth
A wonder crown his faith!
And count ye all both great and small
As numbered with the dead!
For mariner for forty year,
On Erie, boy and man,

I never yet saw such a storm,
Or one't with it began!

So overboard a keg of nails
And anvils three we threw,
Likewise four bales of gunny-sack,
Two hundred pounds of glue,
Two sacks of corn, four ditto wheat,
A box of books, a cow,
A violin, Lord Byron's works,
A rip-saw and a sow.

A curve! a curve! the dangers grow!
"Labbord! — stabbord! — steady! — so! —
Hard-a-port, Dol! — hellum-a-lee!
Haw the head mule! — the aft one gee!
Luff! bring her to the wind!"

For straight a farmer brought a plank, —
(Mysteriously inspired) —
And laying it unto the ship,
In silent awe retired.
Then every sufferer stood amazed
That pilot man before;
A moment stood; then wondering turned,
And speechless walked ashore."[33])

A yet more glaring instance of Mark Twain's violent reaction against the typical poetry of the Romantic era is to be found in one of the short pieces collectively entitled *Information Wanted*, among which, incidentally, further literary satire (on Cooper), as well as the narrative of his first meeting with Artemus Ward in the early sixties were included. The content of the volume points to an early date. This small contribution is called *A Couple of Poems by Twain and Moore*. Here too, we must prefix a few introductory notes on the English literary background.

In its day and ever since, Gray's *Elegy Written in a Country Churchyard* aroused immense admiration and acquired many imitators.[34]) The wistful mood of a quiet summer evening brings back memories of bygone days to the poet, and his imagination turns to those who now rest in their graves, above which the curfew is tolling:

> "The curfew tolls the knell of parting day,
> The lowing herd wind slowly o'er the lea,
> The plowman homeward plods his weary way,
> And leaves the world to darkness and to me.
> . . . . .
> Beneath those rugged elms, that yew-tree's shade,
> Where heaves the turf in many a mould'ring heap,
> Each in his narrow cell for ever laid,
> The rude forefathers of the hamlet sleep."

Of the numerous variations written on this theme, that by the facile Thomas Moore was easily the most popular and the best known. His poem was called *Those Evening Bells* and, like all his verse, it was widely recited, quoted, and sung:

> "Those evening bells, those evening bells!
> How many a tale their music tells
> Of youth and home and that sweet time
> When last I heard their soothing chime.
>
> Those joyous hours are passed away;
> And many a heart, that then was gay,
> Within the tomb now darkling dwells,
> And hears no more those evening bells.
>
> And so 'twill be when I am gone —
> That tuneful peal will still ring on;
> While other bards shall walk these dells,
> And sing your praise, sweet evening bells."[35])

Towards the end of the thirties, Thomas Hood, himself a Romantic poet in the sentimental vein, but also priding himself on his humour, had written a parody on Moore's poem as follows:

"Those Evening Bells

'I'd be a parody.'

Those Evening Bells, those Evening Bells,
How many a tale their music tells,
Of Yorkshire cakes and crumpets prime,
And letters only just in time.

The Muffin-boy has pass'd away,
The Postman gone — and I must pay,
For down below Deaf Mary dwells
And does not hear those Evening Bells.

And so 'twill be when she is gone,
That tuneful peal will still ring on,
And other maids, with timely yells,
Forget to stay those Evening Bells."[36])

There is no conclusive evidence that Mark Twain had read or knew Hood's parody. But it is very probable that such was the case, and that it had inspired him to write a similar parody. In any case, Mark Twain selected *Those Evening Bells* as a suitable specimen of what he considered to be Romantic twaddle and wrote the following parody of the poem. First he prints Moore's version and then his own:

"These annual bills, these annual bills.
How many a song their discord thrills
Of *truck* consumed, enjoyed, forgot,
Since I was skinned by last year's lot.

Those joyous beans are passed away;
Those onions blithe, O where are they?
Once loved, lost, mourned, now *vexing* ills
Your shades troop back in annual bills.

And so 'twill be when I'm aground —
These yearly duns will still go round,
While other bards, with frantic quills,
Shall damn and *damn* these annual bills."[37])

Then we have the sentimental ballads of Romanticism, which related a touching story in an effort to induce hardened human hearts to feel love for their fellow-creatures — thus effecting their conversion — a strategy in which Dickens excelled long after the hey-day of Romanticism proper. The most famed and ill-famed protagonist of such a moral tale was probably the hero of Wordsworth's *Peter Bell*, "the ruffian wild" who was out travelling all alone

> "One beautiful November night,
> When the full moon was shining bright
> Upon the rapid river Swale."

Suddenly, Peter saw "a solitary Ass" on the bank of the river. He wanted to steal the ass; he mounted but failed to move the animal from the spot. Instead, the ass

> "with motion dull,
> Upon the pivot of his skull
> Turned round his long left ear."

To rouse it into action, Peter strikes the ass a heavy blow with his stick, but it only "dropped gently down upon his knees" and "as gently on his side he fell," turning "his shining hazel eye" on Peter, "a mild reproachful look, . . . more tender than severe." Then the ass looked towards the river and gave "three miserable groans." Exasperated, Peter uttered "an impious oath . . . whereat . . . the Ass sent forth

> A long, a clamorous bray."

Peter now catches sight of a grisly form in the river and is horrorstruck:

> "His hat is up — and every hair
> Bristles, and whitens in the moon."

He swoons, but when he wakes he thrusts his staff into the water in order to find and rescue the corpse. Then the ass rises,

"His staring bones all shake with joy,
And close by Peter's side he stands.
While Peter o'er the river bends,
The little Ass his neck extends,
And fondly licks his hands."

When Peter has pulled up out of the water the dead owner of the ass, the latter falls on its knees and motions Peter to mount "Upon the pleased and thankful Ass."

It turns out that the ass has watched four days and nights on the meadow by the river without taking a single mouthful of the savoury grass. Now it trots away towards the home of the drowned man with Peter on its back. He is the victim of contending emotions and strange incidents which work upon his hard nature. At one time he takes out his tobacco-box and knocks on its lid in a "light and careless way," whereupon "The Ass turned round his head and grinned." Peter grins too, for the nonce, but turns serious when he hears a rumbling sound under ground (actually the work of miners) which he believes to be a warning from hell. The vision of his dead wife and the vociferation of a Methodist preacher in a chapel by the way make him feel compunction and remorse and finally he melts into tears. When the ass arrives home, the grief of the dead man's wife and daughter is too much for him:

"His heart is opening more and more:
A holy sense pervades his mind;
He feels what he for human-kind
Has never felt before."

He sits in a trance revolving his past life in his mind, and, when he wakes,

"He lifts his head — and sees the Ass
Yet standing in the clear moonshine;
When shall I be as good as thou?
Oh, would, poor beast, that I had now
A heart but half as good as thine."

When, finally, the little son of the dead man returns from his search and covers the ass with kisses, Peter Bell,

"this ruffian wild,
Sobs loud, he sobs even like a child,
Oh, God, I can endure no more.

. . . . .

And, after ten months melancholy,
Became a good and honest man." [38])

There is no doubt whatever that *Peter Bell* attracted wide and very unfavourable notice at the time of its publication. The ballad at once became the butt of satire directed against Romantic poets' "Christmas stories tortured into rhyme" that "contain the essence of the true sublime." [39]) Many parodies appeared, among which Shelley's *Peter Bell the Third* is the most famous one, though published posthumously in 1839. [40])

This literary *genre* inspired Mark Twain to many humoresques among which the best-known appeared under the title *About Magnanimous Incident Literature*. In the introductory remarks to, the three stories related under the above title, he complains that the moral tales in question always stop at the climax whereas the real interest attaches to the later developments. And so he undertakes to write the sequels of the three samples he has collected for the purpose.

The first tale is headed:

"The Grateful Poodle

One day a benevolent physician (who had read the books) having found a stray poodle suffering from a broken leg, conveyed the poor creature to his home, and, after setting and bandaging the injured limb, gave the little outcast its liberty again, and thought no more about the matter. But how great was his surprise, upon opening his door one morning, some days later, to find the grateful poodle patiently waiting there, and in its company another stray dog, one of whose legs, by accident, had been broken. The kind physician at once relieved the distressed animal, nor did he forget to admire the inscrutable goodness and mercy of God, who had been willing to use so humble an instrument as the poor outcast poodle for the inculcating of, etc. etc. etc.

Sequel

The next morning the benevolent physician found the two dogs beaming with gratitude, waiting at his door, and with them two other dogs, cripples. The cripples were speedily healed, and the four went their way, leaving the benevolent physician more overcome by pious wonder than ever. The day passed, the morning came. There at the door sat now the four reconstructed dogs, and with them four others requiring reconstruction. This day also passed, and another morning came; and now sixteen dogs, eight of them newly crippled, occupied the sidewalk, and the people were going around. By noon the broken legs were all set, but the pious wonder in the good physician's breast was beginning to get mixed with involuntary profanity. The sun rose once more, and exhibited thirty-two dogs, sixteen of them with broken legs, occupying the sidewalk and half of the street; the human spectators took up the rest of the room. The cries of the wounded, the songs of the healed brutes, and the comments of the onlooking citizens made great and inspiring cheer but the traffic was interrupted in that street. The good physician hired a couple of assistant surgeons and got through his benevolent work before dark, first taking the precaution to cancel his church membership, so that he might express himself with the latitude which the case required.

But some things have their limits. When once more the morning dawned, and the good physician looked out upon a massed and far-reaching multitude of clamorous and beseeching dogs, he said, "I might as well acknowledge it, I have been fooled by the books; they only tell the pretty part of the story, and then stop. Fetch me the shot-gun; this thing has gone along far enough."

He issued forth with his weapon and chanced to step upon the tail of the original poodle, who promptly bit him in the leg. Now the great and good work which this poodle had been

engaged in had engendered in him such a mighty and aug-
menting enthusiasm as to turn his weak head at last and drive
him mad. A month later, when the benevolent physician lay in
the death throes of hydrophobia, he called his weeping friends
about him and said:

"Beware of the books. They tell but half of the story.
Whenever a poor wretch asks you for help, and you feel a doubt
as to what result may flow from you benevolence, give yourself
the benefit of the doubt and kill the applicant."

And so saying he turned his face to the wall and gave up
the ghost . . ."[41])

But the heaviest censure from Mark Twain is incurred by
two Romantic writers of world-wide renown, Walter Scott and
Fenimore Cooper. This is in the nature of things, as the grown-
up man is inclined to let the heroes of his youth pay for the
absorbing idolatry they evoked from the child. And that Scott
and Cooper were the idols of the boy Sam Clemens, there is
not the slightest doubt. This much is proved by the intimate
acquaintance with their work which he evinces in numerous
places.

Mark Twain first deals with Scott. He does so in the book
which describes his departure from home as a very young man,
to grapple with life on his own account, *Life on the Mississippi*.
In particular, the earlier chapters of vol. II are devoted to much
abuse of Sir Walter. The sight of the Capitol of Baton Rouge
convinces the spectator that this little sham castle with turrets
and things is due to the debilitating influence of Scott's medieval
romances. It would never have been built if he had not driven
the people mad, a couple of generations ago:

"Sir Walter Scott 'is probably responsible for the Capitol
building; for it is not conceivable that this little sham castle
would ever have been built if he had not run the people mad,
a couple of generations ago, with his medieval romances. The
South has not yet recovered from the debilitating influence of
his books. Admiration of his fantastic heroes and their grotesque
"chivalry" doings and romantic juvenilities still survives here,
in an atmosphere in which is already perceptible the wholesome

and practical nineteenth-century smell of cotton-factories and locomotives; and traces of its inflated language and other windy humbuggeries survive along with it. It is pathetic enough, that a whitewashed castle, with turrets and things, — materials and all ungenuine within and without, pretending to be what they are not — should ever have been built in this otherwise honourable place but it is much more pathetic to see this architectural falsehood undergoing restoration and perpetuation in our day, when it would have been so easy to let dynamite finish what a charitable fire began, and then devote this restoration-money to the building of something genuine."[42])

Later on, when the author gets as far as New Orleans, he finds fault with the English style of Southern newspapermen — and ascribes it to Scott. He relates how the captain of a Mississippi steamer invited some ladies to make a trip with him and what became of this plain event as penned by a newspaperman. The women are termed "the beauty of the place" and the steamer's "fair freight," and they do not pay a visit to the cabin but "grace" it with their presence and make the steamer feel "gallant." The chivalry of Southern men towards women is something ridiculous, and it is all the fault of Sir Walter:

"The 'Times-Democrat' sent a relief-steamer up one of the bayous, last April. This steamer landed at a village, up there somewhere, and the Captain invited some of the ladies of the village to make a short trip with him. They accepted and came aboard, and the steamboat shoved out up the creek. That was all there was 'to it.' And that is all that the editor of the 'Times-Democrat' would have got out of it. There was nothing in the thing but statistics, and he would have got nothing else out of it. He would probably have even tabulated them, partly to secure perfect clearness of statement, and partly to save space. But his special correspondent knows other methods of handling statistics. He just throws off all restraint and vallows in them — 'On Saturday, early in the morning, the beauty of the place graced our cabin, and proud of her fair freight the gallant little boat glided up the bayou.' Twenty-two words to say the ladies came aboard and the boat shoved out up the creek, is a clean waste of ten good words, and is also destructive of compactness of statement. The trouble with the Southern reporter is — Women. They unsettle him; they throw him off his balance. He is plain, and sensible, and satisfactory, until a woman heaves in sight. Then he goes all to pieces; his mind totters, he becomes flowery and idiotic. From reading the above extract, you would imagine that this student of Sir Walter Scott is an apprentice, and knows next to nothing about handling a pen. On the contrary, he furnishes plenty of proof, in his long letter, that he knows well enough how to handle it when the women are not around to give him the artificial-flower complaint."[43])

Relating the incidents of a mule race, which Mark Twain attended at New Orleans together with "the beauty and chivalry" of the place — in the words of the Southern reporter — he returns to the charge. The trouble with these reporters is Women, supplemented by Walter Scott and his knights and beauty and chivalry:

"But let us return to the mule. Since I left him, I have rummaged around and found a full report of the race. In it I find confirmation of the theory which I broached just now — namely, that the trouble with the Southern reporter is Women: Women, supplemented by Walter Scott and his knights and beauty and chivalry, and so on. This is an excellent report, as long as the women stay out of it. But when they intrude, we have this frantic result. —"[44])

And he gives a long extract from the newspaper version of the incident:

"It will probably be a long time before the ladies' stand presents such a sea of foam-like loveliness as it did yesterday. Then New Orleans women are always charming, but never so much so as at this time of the year, when in their dainty spring costumes they bring with them a breath of balmy freshness and an odour of sanctity unspeakable. The stand was so crowded with them that, walking at their feet and seeing no possibility

of approach, many a man appreciated as he never did before
the Peri's feeling at the gates of Paradise, and wondered what
was the priceless boon that would admit him to their sacred
presence. Sparkling on their white-robed breasts or shoulders
were the colours of their favourite knights, and were it not for
the fact that the doughty heroes appeared on unromantic mules,
it would have been easy to imagine one of King Arthus's gala-
days." [45]

Immediately after, he describes the Mardi-Gras festivities and
this description also evokes abuse of Scott. In fact, poor Sir
Walter is always a handy butt. Whereas Mardi-Gras was for-
merly regarded as chiefly of religious origin and bore a corresponding stamp, its features are now regulated by medieval
pageantry filched from the Waverley novels:

"Mardi-Gras is of course a relic of the French and Spanish
occupation; but I judge that the religious feature has been pretty
well knocked out of it now. Sir Walter has got the advantage
of the gentleman of the cowl and rosary, and he will stay. His
medieval business, supplemented by the monsters and oddities,
and the pleasant creatures from fairy-land, is finer to look at
than the poor fantastic inventions and performances of the
revelling rabble of the priest's day, and serves quite as well,
perhaps, to emphasize the day and admonish men that the
grace-line between the worldly season and the holy one is
reached." [46]

This chapter contains the chief onslaught on Scott only a
page later. The Mardi-Gras festivities, Mark Twain says, have
spread from New Orleans towards the North as far as St. Louis
and Baltimore. But farther it cannot go, because its girly-girly
romance would kill it with practical Northerners. To these
reflections the author adds his conviction of the services rendered
to mankind by the French Revolution and Napoleon. They
destroyed the authority of the Church and made us free. And
Napoleon set merit above birth and stripped royalty of its
divinity. All these benefactions are made abortive by Scott.
His sham-medieval civilization has checked the progress of society

and developed into what the author calls the "Sir Walter disease."
The mixture of the modern and medieval which this disease
implies, has set back the South fully a generation, and his crime
is greater than that of slavery (on which everything that is
wrong with the South is otherwise customarily fathered). The
fact that Southern literature has lost irretrievably in quantity
and quality is also due to Scott; but when his influence is a
thing of the past, the South will boast not three or four first-
rate literary men but a dozen or two. What immense good
(or harm) can be wrought by a single book is plainly shown
by two such novels as *Don Quijote* and *Ivanhoe*:

"Then comes Sir Walter Scott with his enchantment, and
by his single might checks this wave of progress, and even
turns it back; sets the world in love with dreams and phantoms;
with decayed and swinish forms of religion; with decayed and
degraded systems of government; with the silliness and emp-
tiness, sham grandeurs, sham gauds, and sham chivalries of a
brainless and worthless long-vanished society. He did measure-
less harm; more real and lasting harm, perhaps than any other
individual that ever wrote. Most of the world has now outlived
good part of these harms, though by no means all of them;
but in our South they flourish pretty forcefully still. Not so
forcefully as half a generation ago; perhaps, but still forcefully.
There the genuine and wholesome civilisation of the nineteenth
century is curiously confused and commingled with the Walter
Scott Middle-Age sham civilisation; and so you have practical,
common-sense, progressive works, mixed up with the duel, the
inflated speech, and the jejune romanticism of an absurd past
that is dead, and out of charity ought to be buried. But for
the Sir Walter Scott disease, the character of the Southerner —
or Southron, according to Sir Walter's starchier way of phrasing
it — would be wholly modern, in place of modern and medieval
mixed, and the South would be fully a generation further advanced than it is. It was Sir Walter that made every gentleman
in the South a Major, or a Colonel, or a General, or a Judge,
before the war; and it was he, also, that made these gentlemen
value these bogus decorations. For it was he that created rank

and caste down there, and also reverence for rank and caste, and
pride and pleasure in them. Enough is said on slavery, without
fathering upon it these creations and contributions of Sir Walter.
Sir Walter had so large a hand in making Southern character,
as it existed before the war, that he is in great measure responsible for the war. It seems a little harsh toward a dead
man to say that we never should have had any war but for
Sir Walter; and yet something of a plausible argument might,
perhaps, be made in support of that wild proposition. The
Southerner of the American Revolution owned slaves; so did
the Southerner of the Civil War: but the former resembles the
latter as an Englishman resembles a Frenchman. The change
of character can be traced rather more easily to Sir Walter's
influence than to that of any other thing or person.

One may observe, by one or two signs, how deeply that
influence penetrated, and how strongly it holds. If one take up
a Northern or Southern literary periodical of forty or fifty years
ago, he will find it filled with wordy, windy, flowery 'eloquence,'
romanticism, sentimentality — all imitated from Sir Walter, and
sufficiently badly done, too — innocent travesties of his style
and methods, in fact. This sort of literature being the fashion
in both sections of the country, there was opportunity for the
fairest competition; and as a consequence, the South was able
to show as many well-known literary names, proportioned to
population, as the North could do.

But a change has come, and there is no opportunity now
for a fair competition between North and South. For the North
has thrown out that old inflated style, whereas the Southern
writer still clings to it — clings to it and has a restricted market
for his wares, as a consequence. There is as much literary
talent in the South, now, as ever there was, of course; but its
work can gain but slight currency under present conditions;
the authors write for the past, not the present; they use ob-
solete forms, and a dead language. But when a Southerner of
genius writes modern English, his book goes upon crutches no
longer, but upon wings; and they carry it swiftly all about
America and England, and through the great English reprint
publishing houses of Germany — as witness the experience of

Mr. Cable and Uncle Remus, two of the very few Southern authors who do not write in the Southern style. Instead of three or four widely-known literary names, the South ought to have a dozen or two — and will have them when Sir Walter's time is out.

A curious exemplification of the power of a single book for good or harm is shown in the effects wrought by Don Quixote and those wrought by Ivanhoe. The first swept the world's admiration for the medieval chivalry silliness out of existence; and the other restored it. As far as our South is concerned, the good work done by Cervantes is pretty nearly a dead letter, so effectually has Scott's pernicious work undermined it."[47])

This is rather a heavy charge. But still, Mark Twain finds even more fault with Cooper, whom he evidently studied so closely that many entire pages remained in his memory the whole of his life. In any case, he objects to Cooper's admirers like Lounsbury, Brander Matthews, and Wilkie Collins, stating that they have no right to deliver opinions on Cooper, a right which he thinks belongs only to those who have acquired real familiarity with the *Leatherstocking* absurdities. In the latter category, Mark Twain preeminently places himself.

In the elaborate essay, *Fenimore Cooper's Literary Offences*, Mark Twain acts as literary critic for once, a fact which is rather significant from our point of view. Otherwise, he loved to pose as the unliterary man or even *ignoramus* in such matters, a fact which has deceived most of his own critics.[48]) In this essay, he finds that, in barely two-thirds of a page of *The Deerslayer*, its author has scored 114 offences against literary art out of a possible 115. In Mark Twain's opinion, this novel has no logical plot, shows complete mismanagement of the episodes, and contains only unnatural personages: These do not belong to the tale organically, they do not talk like human beings, their character is out of keeping with their actions and words, their conversation begins in the pure Sunday School style and ends in Negro minstrelsy, their stupidity is called the craft of the woodman, they achieve impossible miracles instead of natural actions, they are thoroughly hateful to the reader, though intended by Cooper to be winning, they always do the logically wrong thing, etc.

In addition, Cooper is accused of never saying what he wants to say, of never hitting upon the right word, of omitting necessary particulars, of incurring slovenliness in form, of using bad grammar, of lacking simple and straightforward style, and other things.

Further, Cooper's inventiveness is called into question. He has only six or eight tricks for his savages and woodmen to deceive each other, *viz.* to tread in the tracks of an enemy in order to hide one's own trail, to step on a dry twig when surrounded by dangers (Mark Twain thinks the *Leatherstocking Series* ought rather to be called the *Broken Twig Series*), and so on.

Then, Mark Twain gives concrete instances of Cooper's ridiculous mistakes, as he thinks. He mentions the incident of the "undertow" in *The Pathfinder* when Jasper Eau-douce saves *The Scud* on Lake Ontario. He lists the incidents in *The Last of the Mohicans* when the scout has lost his way in the fog and a cannon-ball comes rolling to his feet showing him the direction towards Fort William Henry; when Chingachgook turns a running stream out of its course and finds the tracks of the person he is looking for; the episode in the caves and the fight with Magua; Deerslayer's killing of his first Indian and his soliloquy over the corpse; the description of the outlet of Lake Glimmerglass in *The Deerslayer*; the attack of the Indians on the Ark in that outlet; the shooting-match in *The Pathfinder*, and so on.

Finally, he states that Cooper's word-sense is doubtful or "dull." And he supports his opinion by lengthily enumerating words culled from half a dozen pages of *The Deerslayer* which Cooper has used in a wrong sense, since he meant to say something quite different from what he actually has said. And the essay ends with a statement that *The Deerslayer* is "just simply a literary *delirium tremens*."

The summary reads like this:

"A work of art? It has no invention; it has no order, system, sequence, or result; it has no lifelikeness, no thrill, no stir, no seeming of reality; its characters are confusedly drawn, and by their acts and words they prove that they are not the sort of people the author claims that they are; its humour is pathetic; its pathos is funny; its conversations are — oh, indescribable; its lovescenes odious; its English a crime against the language. Counting these out, what is left is Art. I think we must all admit that."

After this severe verdict, it would require no little ingeniousness on Mark Twain's part to account for the fact that Cooper is one of the most widely read authors in the world and that his readers are not confined to the uneducated or unlettered.

Before we pursue the subject Mark Twain v. Cooper any further, we must once more recall some facts of literary history.

Among the chief formative factors in the history of European Romanticism is the publication of Macpherson's *Ossian*. As is well known, this is the collective title of several epics in rhythmical prose — *Fingal*, *Temora*, etc. — of which Macpherson professed to be the editor, not the author, and which appeared between 1760 and 1765. The collective title took its name from one of the chief characters in these epics, the blind and aged bard Ossian. *Ossian* describes the heroic age of the Celtic people — primitive, but set in sublime and awe-inspiring scenery. The deeds in battle of the heroes were always "mighty" verging on the supernatural, the courage manifested, the strength, the agility, the endurance, the magnanimity or malevolence outdid Homer. The style and language of the epics were high-flown and high-sounding. It was intended to be the adequate expression of a primitive elemental mind. A brooding melancholy and sadness hovered over the whole, together with an obtrusive sense of fallen greatness and departed glory. Repeated genealogical references presupposed the reader's acquaintance with the great and mighty of a perished race:

"Cuchullin sat by Tura's well, by the tree of the rustling sound. His spear leaned against the rock . . . Amid his thoughts of mighty Cairbar, a hero slain by the chief in war, the scout of ocean comes, Moran, the son of Fithil . . . He sat on the shore like a cloud of mist on the silent hill . . . Who in this

land appears like me? . . . Who can meet Swaran in fight? . . .
Let dark Cuchullin yield to him, that is strong as the storms
of his land . . . Strike the sounding shield of Semo . . . The
sound of peace is not its voice . . . My heroes shall hear and obey
. . . Now I behold the chiefs, in the pride of their former deeds.
Their souls are kindled at the battles of old . . . Their eyes
are flames of fire. They roll in search of the foes of the land.
Their mighty hands are on their swords . . . Bright are the chiefs
of battle . . . Gloomy and dark their heroes follow . . . Hail,
sons of the narrow vales; hail, hunters of the deer . . . Go,
Connal, to thy silent hills, . . . pursue the dark-brown deer of
Cromla; stop with thine arrows bounding roes of Lean. But,
blue-eyed son of Semo, . . . Ruler of the field . . . scatter thou
the sons of Lochlin, roar thou of the ranks of their pride."[49])

"Where is the son of Selma; he who led in war? I behold
not his steps, among my people, returning from the field. Fell
the young bounding roe, who was stately on the hills? He fell,
for ye are silent . . . Cathmore . . . remembers the falling away
of the people. They come, a stream, are rolled away, another
race succeeds. But some mark the fields, as they pass, with
their own mighty names . . . Of these be the chief of Atha . . .
Often may the voice of future times meet Cathmor in the air,
when he strides from wind to wind, or folds himself in the wing
of a storm . . . Why is the king so sad? said Mathos eagle-eyed.
Remains there a foe at Lubar? . . . Not so peaceful was thy
father . . . His rage was a fire that always burned, his joy over
fallen foes was great . . . His name remains in Atha, like the
awful memory of ghosts, whose presence was terrible . . . Where
art thou, beam of light? Hunters from the mossy rock, saw ye
the blue eyed fair? Are her steps on grassy Lumon, near the
bed of the roses? Ah me, I behold her bow in the hall."[50])

"Such were my deeds, son of Alpin, when the arm of my
youth was strong . . . My voice is like the last sound of the
wind, when it forsakes the woods . . . The sons of feeble men
shall behold me and admire the statue of the chiefs of old . . .
for my steps shall be in the clouds . . . The aged oak bends
over the stream. It sighs with all its moss. The withered fern

whistles near and mixes, as it waves, with Ossian's hair . . .
Thou takest the sun in thy wrath and hidest him in thy clouds.
The sons of little men are afraid . . . We passed away . . . our
departure was in renown . . . The life of Ossian fails . . . My
steps are not seen in Selma . . . But why are thou sad, son of
Fingal? Why grows the cloud of thy soul? The chiefs of other
times are departed . . . Another race shall arise. The people
are like the waves of the ocean: like the leaves of woody
Morven, they shall pass away in the rustling blast and other
leaves lift their green heads on high. Did thy beauty last, O
Ryno? Stood the strength of car-borne Oscar? Fingal himself
departed. The hall of his fathers forgot his steps. Shalt thou
remain, thou aged bard, when the mighty have failed?"[51])

As far as I am aware, it has escaped the attention of scholars
that *Ossian* acquired an ardent admirer in Cooper, as earlier in
Chateaubriand.[52]) There can be no doubt whatever that the
author of the *Leatherstocking Tales* looked upon the declining
race of the Red Man in terms of the by-gone heroic age of
Fingal and Cuchullin.[53]) His heroes Tamenund, Chingachgook,
Uncas, and other Indian chiefs all speak the high-flown language
of *Ossian*. When Chingachgook speaks of himself — or for
that matter Tamenund, Uncas, Magua, etc. — he does not say
"I" but "Chingachgook" (Tamenund, Uncas, Magua), just as
Ossian says "Ossian," not "I," when speaking of himself. The
boasting is identical, likewise the pride of race, the lust for
cruelty and blood, the reviling of the enemy, and the keen
awareness of nature. The wise and melancholy words of Tamenund might be those of the aged Ossian himself. The deep
gloom of the last chapter and the death of Uncas in *The Last
of the Mohicans* are expressed in pure Ossianese. The long-
bounding warrior of Macpherson's epic is actually a "Cerf Agile"
like Uncas, in old age he is a withered oak both in Ossian and
among the Delawares. The metaphors used by the Celtic heroes
are closely akin to those employed by the Indian chiefs:

"My pale-face friend is right. A cloud came over the face
of Chingachgook and weakness got into his mind while his eyes
were dim . . . One of my prisoners is a great warrior, tall as a

pine, strong as the moose, active as a deer, fierce as the panther.
Some day he'll be great chief . . . Why should Rivenoak and
his brother leave any cloud between them? They are both wise,
both brave, and both generous. They ought to part friends." [54])
"Chingachgook has seen them. An old man and a young
warrior — the falling hemlock and the tall pine . . . The trees
were too many and the leaves covered their boughs like clouds
hiding the heavens in a storm. But Chingachgook heard the
laugh of Wah-ta-Wah; he knew it from the laugh of the women
of the Iroquois. It sounded in his ears like the chirp of the
wren." [55]) "My old father and my young brother, The Great
Pine, want to see Huron scalps at their belts . . . There is room
for some on the girdle of the Serpent, and his people will look
for them when he goes back to his village. Their eyes must
not be left long in a fog, but they must see what they look
for. I know that my brother has a white hand. He will not
strike even the dead. He will wait for us. When we come
back, he will not hide his face in shame for his friend. The
Great Serpent of the Mohicans must be worthy to go on the
war-path with Hawkeye." [56])

"I know that the pale-faces are a proud and hungry race.
I know that they claim, not only to have the earth, but that the
meanest of their colour is better than Sachems of the red man . . .
But let them not boast before the face of Manitto too loud . . .
I have often seen the locusts strip the leaves from the trees, but
the season of blossoms has always come again." [57])

"I have lived to see the tribes of the Lenape driven from
their council-fires, and scattered like broken herds of deer among
the hills of the Iroquois. I have seen the hatchets of a strange
people sweep the woods from the valleys, that the wind of
heaven had spared. The beasts that run on the mountains, and
the birds that fly above the trees, have I seen living in the
wigwams of men: . . . Does Tamenund dream? What voice is
at his ear? Have the winters gone backward? Will summer
come again to the children of the Lenape? . . . Men of the Leni
Lenape, my race upholds the earth. Your feeble tribes stand
on my shell . . . My race is the grandfather of nations . . . The

hour of Tamenund is nigh! The day has come, at last, to the
night. I thank the Manitto, that one is here to fill my place
at the council fire. Uncas, the child of Uncas, is found. Let
the eyes of a dying eagle gaze on the rising sun . . . The arrow
of Tamenund would not frighten the young fawn, his arm is
withered like the branch of the dying oak, the snail would be
swifter in the race. Yet is Uncas before him as they went to
battle against the pale-faces. Uncas, the panther of the tribe,
the eldest son of the Lenape, the wisest Sagamore of the
Mohicans. Tell me, ye Delawares, has Tamenund been a sleeper
for a hundred winters?"[58])

"Why hast thou left us, pride of the Wapanachi? . . . Thy
time has been like that of the sun when in the trees. Thy glory
brighter than is light at noon-day. Thou art gone, youthful
warrior, but a hundred Wyandots are clearing the briars from
thy path to the world of spirits. Who that saw thee in battle
would believe that thou couldst die? Who, before thee, has
ever shown Uttawa the way into the fight? Thy feet were like
the wings of eagles. Thine arm heavier than falling branches
from the pine. And thy voice like the Manitto, when he speaks
in the clouds. The tongue of Uttawa is weak and his heart is
exceeding heavy. Pride of the Wapanachi, why hast thou left
us? . . . It is enough. Go, children of the Lenape. The anger
of the Manitto is not done. Why should Tamenund stay? . . .
my day has been too long. In the morning I saw the sons of
Unamis happy and strong, and yet before the night has come
have I lived to see the last warrior of the wise race of the
Mohicans."[59])

When, now, Mark Twain attacked the language which Cooper
puts into the mouth of the Red Man, he selected a weak spot
which had already attracted the attention of critics. Reviewers
had pointed out that this was the language of civilized men
expressed and transformed by a poet. But what they did not
see was that Cooper had not invented this style, but was only
subjected to the influence of Romanticism in one of its most
contagious forms.

Whether Mark Twain wanted to ridicule *Ossian* when he

attacked Cooper's language, we have no means of knowing. I
cannot think he did, even if he knew the Celtic epic in question.
It was enough for him that the expressions of Uncas, Chingachgook, Tamenund, and so on, were unnatural and bombastic.

In any case, when he wrote his little sketch called *Niagara*,
he tilted against this literary sin in particular of Cooper's and
made the narrator speak to the Indians in a way calculated to
give a fair sample of Cooper's stylistic blunders.

The sketch called *Niagara* was written in or about 1871.
When the narrator arrived at the famous spot and saw the
shops full of moccasins, Indian dolls and the like, he expected
to meet the Red Man in the neighbourhood and his expectancy
rose to a high pitch, because he had always admired the Indian
as described in the romances of Cooper:

"The noble Red Man has always been a friend and darling
of mine. I love to read about him in tales and legends and
romances. I love to read of his inspired sagacity, and his love
of the wild free life of mountain and forest, and his general
nobility of character, and his stately metaphorical manner of
speech, and his chivalrous love for the dusky maiden, and the
picturesque pomp of his dress and accoutrement."

But the first specimen of the race he met and addressed,
turned out to be an Irishman in Indian attire who resented
very much being taken for a Red Man. The same was the
case when he came across a "dusky maiden, the Pride of the
Forest." She is just as abusive as her fellowcountryman, the
Indian Irishman. And when, finally, he runs into an Indian
camp and makes a speech to the savages gathered there, in the
flowery language of *The Deerslayer* and *The Last of the Mohicans,* they are on the point of killing him and finally throw
him into the cataract.

The narrator addresses the Indian maiden in this way:

"Is the heart of the forest maiden heavy? Is the Laughing
Tadpole lonely? Does she mourn over the extinguished
council-fires of her race, and the vanished glory of her ancestors? Or does her sad spirit wander afar towards the

hunting-grounds whither her brave Gobbler-of-the-Lightnings is gone? Why is my daughter silent? Has she aught against the pale-face stranger?"

And these are his words to "the noble Son of the Forest:"

"Is the Wawhoo-Wang-Wang of the Wack-a-Whack happy? Does the great Speckled Thunder sigh for the war-path, or is his heart contented with dreaming of the dusky maiden, the Pride of the Forest? Does the mighty Sachem yearn to drink the blood of his enemies, or is he satisfied to make bead reticules for the papooses of the pale-face? Speak, sublime relic of by-gone grandeur — venerable ruin, speak."

And lastly, he spoke to the Indian camp as follows:

"Noble Red Men, Braves, Grand Sachems, War Chiefs, Squaws, and High Muck-a-Mucks, the paleface from the land of the setting sun greets you. You, Beneficent Polecat — you, Devourer of Mountains — you, Roaring Thundergusts — you, Bully Boy with a Glass Eye — the paleface from beyond the great waters greets you all. War and pestilence have thinned your ranks, and destroyed your once proud nation. Poker and seven-up, and a vain modern expense for soap, unknown to your glorious ancestors, have depleted your purses. Appropriating, in your simplicity, the property of others, has gotten you into trouble. Misrepresenting facts, in your simple innocence, has damaged your reputation with the soulless usurper. Trading for forty-rod whisky, to enable you to get drunk and happy and tomahawk your families, has played the everlasting mischief with the picturesque pomp of your dress, and here you are, in the broad light of the 19th century, gotten up like the ragtag-and-bobtail of the purlieus of New York. For shame, recall your ancestors. Recall their mighty deeds. Remember Uncas — and Red Jacket — and Hole-in-the-Day — and Whoopde-doodledo. Emulate their achievements. Unfurl yourselves under my banner, noble savages, illustrious guttersnipes."[60])

His most elaborate and sustained attack on Romanticism is to be found in the novel *A Connecticut Yankee at the Court of King Arthur*. The aim of the book is to show that the Middle

Ages, which Scott had described as instinct with high ideals, chivalry, refinement, and truth, actually constituted a period of ignorance, crime, low culture, deficient hygiene, superstition, and boorishness. The King was no exception, his knights were of a piece with him. The shrewd yankee who is placed in the surroundings of the Middle Ages, has cleaner personal habits, is more just, and has a more truly Christian notion of justice and social welfare. He is of course much more gifted, and the miracles which famous sorcerers like Merlin achieve fall to the ground before him. The archaic language which Scott put into the mouths of his characters is exposed to heavy ridicule by Mark Twain. As a very apt illustration of his way of satirizing Scott's medieval apparatus, we may quote the passage describing the Stylite:

"His stand was a pillar 60 feet high, with a broad platform on the top of it. He was . . . bowing his body ceaselessly and rapidly almost to his feet . . . I timed him with a stop-watch, and he made 1244 revolutions in 24 minutes and 46 seconds . . . I made a note in my memorandum-book, purposing some day to apply a system of elastic chords to him and run a sewing-machine with it. I afterwards carried out that scheme, and got five years' good service out of him; in which time he turned out upwards of 18,000 first-rate tow-linen shirts, which was ten a day. I worked him Sundays and all; he was going Sundays the same as week-days, and it was no use to waste the power. These shirts . . . sold like smoke to the pilgrims at 1.50 doll. They were . . . advertised . . . everywhere . . . inasmuch as there was not a cliff . . . in England but you could read on it at a mile distance:

"Buy the only genuine St Stylite; patronized by the No-bility. Patent applied for." "[61])

In view of the material presented here, there can be no doubt of the fact that we find an aggressive reaction against Romanticism in the literature of the United States; in fact, as aggressive as that which meets the eye in the work of Thackeray and others in English letters. It is further evident from our material that Mark Twain was a literary man who took a strong interest in belles-lettres, and that he represented the transatlantic reaction against Romanticism with more consistency, violence, and success than any of his contemporaries.

On this subject we must disagree even with a scholar of Parrington's standing. He does not claim to have intended to write a history of American literature. Nevertheless, there is no denying that, time and time again, he shifts his standpoint from the social to the literary field. We cannot, like him, ascribe the phenomenon of Mark Twain to the overriding influence of the Middle West on American letters. He was neither unlettered nor uncouth, as Parrington, in his endeavour to fit in Mark Twain into his system, seems to imply. *Materially*, he was not changed by that New England polish which Parrington seems to think was so essential to him. If he had been even vestigially a literary tyro, he would not have been attracted to Olivia Langdon and her New England atmosphere with its implications of friendships and conservative literary ideals. If we are content to interpret him in this comfortable way, we cannot account for this literary work at all, nor for his life in general. We have evidence of his literary readings and inclinations as a boy; already in his teens he published a parody of *The Burial of Sir John Moore* (Mark Twain claims to have been only thirteen at the time).[62]) At that early age he absorbed Scott and Cooper as eagerly as any other adventurous lad, but in such a way as to be able to turn his readings to literary account later on. The publication, in 1938, of his letters from the Sandwich Islands with the accompanying introduction by G. E. Dane shows us the picture of a cultured and *literary* man. *The Innocents Abroad*, published not long after the trip to the Sandwich Islands, does so too. Chapter VII of his *Note-Book* testifies to the fact that he saw *essential* Greece with its monuments and memories, just as the most cultured European traveller might have done. Such was also the case, judging from the *Note-Book*, with Palestine, Egypt, and other Mediterranean countries with a remote past which he visited of this memorable trip.

A still more important proof of his essential mental refinement, culture, and poetic sense of values, is *Joan of Arc*. This subject is, and always was, an important test-case. Mark Twain is generally regarded as having stood the test with eminent success.

Another important fact which has been overlooked is that he would not have subjected himself to that severe apprenticeship in literary expression (of which he has given an amusing account) had he not possessed strong literary aspirations. He would not have entered upon a detailed *literary* criticism of Cooper, if he had not had *literary* ideals and ideas himself. He would not have bothered so much about the poets and novelists he attacked, directly or indirectly, if he had not felt himself a member of their brotherhood. We note that, even in the case of Scott, he did not only attack the spirit but also the literary form of the Waverley Novels. Finally, were we to accept the picture of Mark Twain which we have tried to expose as unsatisfactory, we ought not to reject an identical image of Bret Harte. Both men were in the same boat as regards their claims to literary status in America.

As a matter of fact, it is difficult to imagine that anyone could regard Mark Twain even for a moment as a literary buffoon, now that we have access to his own *Autobiography*, with its delicate portraits of his mother and his friends — and of himself, of that sensitive boy with the carefully assumed care-free face. To all that subscribe to the Middle-Westerner-pioneer theory about him, we should like to repeat the closing lines of the *Preface as from the Dead* which he prefixed to that *Autobiography*:

"It has seemed to me that I could be as frank and free and unembarrassed as a love letter if I knew that what I was writing would be exposed to no eye until I was dead, and unaware, and indifferent."

Abbreviations.

A	= Anglia,
ABl	= Anglia Beiblatt.
AStNSp	= Archiv für das Studium der neueren Sprachen.
CHAL	= The Cambridge History of American Literature.
CHEL	= The Cambridge History of English Literature.
ed.	= edition.
edd.	= editions.

ESt	= Englische Studien.
GRM	= Germanisch-Romanische Monatsschrift.
JEGPh	= Journal of English and Germanic Philology.
MLN	= Modern Language Notes.
MLR	= The Modern Language Review.
MPh	= Modern Philology.
N	= Neophilologus.
PhQu	= The Philological Quarterly.
PMLA	= The Publications of the Modern Language Association of America.
R	= Routledge edition.
RLC	= Revue de littérature comparée.
StPh	= Studies in Philology (Chapel Hill).
T	= Tauchitz Edition.
vol.	= volume.
vols.	= volumes.

The present essay refers to the *Author's National Edition* in 25 vols., where not otherwise indicated.

Notes.

1. Carl Van Doren, *American Literature. An Introduction*, 1933.
2. *Op. cit.*, p. 9.
3. Some interesting information on this subject is to be found in J. C. McCloskey, *The Campaign of Periodicals after the War of 1812 for National American Literature*, PMLA, 1935, pp. 262 ff. Cf. also E. Mertner, *Zur Theorie der Short Story in England und Amerika*, A, 1941, p. 188 and Note 3; R. Blankenship, *American Literature as an Expression of the National Mind*, 1931.
4. Cf. also some valuable information in W. B. Cairns, *British Republication of American Writings, 1783—1833*. PMLA, 1928, pp. 303 ff.; S. T. Richards, *Longfellow in England*. PMLA, 1936, pp. 1123 ff.
5. A. Compton-Rickett, *A History of English Literature*, 1918. Cf. the handbooks of Brooke-Sampson (*English Literature*, 1935), Legouis-Cazamian (*A History of English Literature* I—II, 1927), Legouis (*A Short History of English Literature*, 1942), Ifor Evans (*A Short History of English Literature*, 1944), Schirmer (*Geschichte der englischen Literatur*, 1937), Sampson (*The Concise CHEL*, 1944), and many others, where there is nothing about American literature. The *CHEL* (XIII, 574) has a bibliography of Henry James, because he is considered to be formally an Englishman, but leaves it to American scholars to write the *CHAL*. Harold Williams has a short *Note on American Novelists* in his *Modern English Writers*, 1918, and later edd., and both he and Fehr (*Englische Literatur des 19./20. Jhdts.*, 1923) include obvious writers like Harland when dealing with *The Yellow Book*.
6. S. B. Liljegren, *American and European in the Works of Henry James*, 1920; J. W. Beach, *The Method of Henry James*, 1918; C. P. Kelley, *The Early Development of Henry James*, 1930 (extensive bibliography); M.-R. Garnier, *Henry James et la France*, 1927; Lotte Borchers, *Frauencharaktere und Frauenprobleme bei Henry James*, 1929 (extensive bibliography).

My statement of the lack of interest in Henry James *on the part of English scholars* does not, as a matter of course, amount to an accusation of indifference on the part of *English readers* towards his work. Numerous notices and reviews in essays and periodicals show the injustice of a similar accusation. Cf. *e. g.* Dixon Scott (*Men of Letters*, 1923), Follett & Follett (*Some Modern Novelists*, 1919, Amer.), C. F. Mc Inture (*PMLA, XX,* Amer.), *The Academy,* 1888, I, 406; 1898, I, 580; II, 169, 338; 1900, II, 260; 1901, I, 165, 308, etc. In addition, see my paper on *Neuere Literatur von und über Henry James, ESt,* LV, 128 ff., and my review of Kelley, *The Early Development of Henry James, MPh,* 1933.

7. G. S. Gordon, *Anglo-American Literary Relations,* 1942, p. 11; cf. *MLR,* 1943, pp. 155 f.

8. If we except George Gordon's six lectures in University College, London, in 1931.

9. See *e. g.* Gordon, *Anglo-American Literary Relations,* pp. 20, 26 f.; B. Fay, *L'esprit revolutionnaire en France et aux États-Unis à la fin du XVIIIe siècle* & *Bibliography,* 1925; P. Valkhoff, *De betekenis van Amerika en Azie voor het West-Europese gedachtleven van de zenventiende en achtiende eeuw, N,* 1938, p. 101 ff.

10. Further orientation *e. g.* in K. Cambell, *Recent Additions to American Literary History, StPh,* 1936, pp. 534 ff.

11. On Cooper I shall quote some passages from J. F. Ross's study on *The Social Criticism of Fenimore Cooper,* 1933: "There was little chance that Cooper would fall under any new literary influence during his years in Europe. The Romantic Movement might be in process of decay, but there is no evidence that Cooper was aware of its passing ... It would seem, then, that there was little European influence on Cooper as a novelist." (p. 53 f.). We shall presently see how erroneous this opinion actually is.

Cf. also *op. cit.,* pp. 20 ff. (the development of Cooper's mind) and pp. 47 ff. (Cooper's early romances); G. Paine, *Cooper and the North American Review,* Royster Memorial Studies, 1931, p. 267 ff.; *ABl,* 1932, p. 347; 1934, p. 348; 1937, p. 83; 1939, p. 251.

12. Cf. *CHAL* I: VIII, where Prof. Goddard speaks of Transcendentalism as a phase of a world-wide movement, but, in my opinion, overstresses the importance of Channing and of the discovery of Germany by Bancroft, Everett, and Ticknor. Cf. also *ESt,* LVI, 172 ff.; A. S. Hill, *The Influence of Emerson,* Harvard Studies and Notes in Philology and Literature, 1896, V, pp. 23—29; E. H. Zeydel, *G. Ticknor and L. Tieck, PMLA,* 1929, pp. 879 ff.

13. W. Fischer, *Die englische Literatur der Vereinigten Staaten von Nordamerika,* pp. 47—48. That Fischer has overlooked some aspect of international literary relationships is evident from the complete severance he makes between Chas Brockden Brown and Cooper, on the one hand, and the statement that American Romanticism — as far as recognized by Fischer — is optimistic, not pessimistic like the European movement. The gloom and tragedy hovering over *The Last of the Mohicans* or *Edgar Huntley* cannot be outdone by any European Romanticist, in my opinion. Cf. also A. O. Lovejoy, *Optimism and Romanticism. PMLA,* 1927, pp. 921 ff.

I might draw attention to the fact that Brockden Brown wrote earlier than Cooper and is, in some respects, akin to Cooper in matter and manner. We have evidence that the question of indebtedness was broached at an early date. In her *Pages and Pictures* published in the opening years of the sixties, Susan Fenimore Cooper tried to vindicate the thesis that *The Last of the Mohicans* was indebted neither to Brockden Brown nor to Chateaubriand:

"In Europe the book produced quite a startling effect; the freshness of the subject, in the sense of fiction, naturally adding greatly to the vivid interest of the narrative. As yet, there had been but one American work of the imagination in which the red man was introduced with any prominence: "Edgar Huntley" by Brockden Brown, a writer of undoubted talent, but scarcely known in England. While alluding to this work, it may be well to remark that Mr. Cooper had not read "Edgar Huntley" since his own boyhood, when his writing an Indian romance himself would have seemed an event wildly improbable. Of the books of Brockden Brown, "Wieland" had made the deepest impression on his mind. "The Mohicans" would assuredly have been precisely the book it now is had "Edgar Huntley" never been written. "The Atala" of M. de Chateaubriand he never read; it was precisely the kind of book in which he would never have felt the least interest, quite too far removed from the realities of life for him to read more than a page or two. To the particular merits of that kind of book he was perhaps scarcely capable of doing justice; he would have lacked the patience to look for them and pages so little in harmony with his own nature." Quoted in M. Clavel, *Fenimore Cooper and His Critics*, 1938, pp. 325 f.; Cf. *ABl*, 1939, pp. 151 ff. Cf. also E. Marchand, *The Literary Opinions of Chas Brockden Brown, StPh*, 1934, 541 ff.; A. Perdeck, *Realism in Modern American Fiction, N*, 1931, p. 118; P. Hazard, *Chateaubriand et la littérature des États-Unis, RLC*, 1928, pp. 46 ff.

14. This statement refers to *literature*. As to *ideas*, see *e.g.* C. H. Faust, *The Background of the Unitarian Opposition to Transcendentalism, MPh*, 1938, pp. 297 ff.

15. On the Pantisocracy scheme of the Lake poets, see J. R. Gillivray, *The Pantisocracy Scheme and Its Immediate Background*, Studies in English, Univ. College of Toronto, 1931, pp. 131—69.

16. Cf. *CHAL*, I, 334 ff.; H. R. Warfel, *Margaret Fuller and R. W. Emerson, PMLA*, 1930, pp. 576 ff.; J. T. Flanagan, *Emerson as a Literary Critic, PhQu*, 1936, pp. 30 ff.

17. Granted Cooper's Romanticism I should like to draw attention to a fact which has so far escaped the notice of scholars, *viz.* the dress of David Gamut in *The Last of the Mohicans*. This dress is actually in the main a variation of Werther's famous dress: blue frock-coat and yellow trousers: "The illassorted and injudicious attire of the individual only served to render his awkwardness more conspicious; a sky-blue coat, with short and broad skirts and low cape, exposed a long thin neck, and longer and thinner legs to the worst animadversions of the evil disposed. His nether garment was of yellow nankeen, closely fitted to the shape, and tied at his bunches of knees by large knots of white ribbon, a good deal sullied by use." It does not seem improbable to me that this trait is a conscious concession to Romanticism on the part of Cooper. Though it *may* also be something which he absorbed unthinkingly from Romantic literature. Other possibilities are, of course, that Gamut's dress only resembled Werther's by chance or was copied from something Cooper had actually seen, though these alternatives seem less probable to me in view of Cooper's rigid allegiance to Romanticism.

There are several other facts which afford surprising insight into the way Cooper's literary manner was shaped by Romanticism. Among the less obvious, and therefore unnoticed, passages of this kind is that in *The Deerslayer* where he traces the origin of the Gothic style to the formation found in woods untouched by man: "The arches of the woods, even at high noon, cast their sombre shadows on the spot which the brilliant rays of the sun that struggled through the leaves contributed to mellow, and, if such an expression can be used, to illuminate. It was probably from a similar scene that the mind of man first got its idea of the effects of Gothic tracery and churchly hues, this temple of nature producing some such effect so far as light and shadows were concerned, as the well-known offspring of human invention." (Ch. XXVII.) — Cf. also Ross, *Op. cit.*, pp. 24, 45, 51, 54, etc.; K. R. Arndt, *New Letters from J. F. Cooper, MLN*, 1937, pp.

117 ff.; J. Routh, *The Model of the Leatherstocking Tales*, *MLN*, 1913, pp. 77 ff.; F. Baldensperger, *Les États-Unis dans la vie et les idées d'Alfred de Vigny*, *RLC*, 1923, pp. 616 ff.

18. The expression is coined by Mark Twain.

19. See *e.g. CHAL*, III: XI *(The Later Novel: Howells)*. Parrington repeatedly refuses to have his work regarded as a sort of literary history, but nevertheless the titles of vols. II and III of his *Main Currents* might be taken to convey his statement of the problem Romanticism-Realism. But his business with Mark Twain, pp. 86 ff., is not a literary analysis, or, where it is, I cannot agree with it; his pages on Howells (241 ff.) are as little satisfactory from my point of view.

20. Cf. Stuart P. Sherman, in *CHAL*, III: VIII; Fischer, p. 107; F. Schönemann, *Mark Twains Weltanschauung*, *ESt*, LV, pp. 53 f., where the thesis is developed that Europe painted a truer picture of Clemens than the U. S. A., an argument which does not convince me; F. Schönemann, *Mr Samuel Langhorne Clemens*, *AStNSp*, 144, 184 ff., where the picture is completed by means of the new edition of his letters; F. Schönemann, *Amerikanischer Humor* I, *GRM*, VIII: 152—164; F. Schönemann, *Mark Twain als literarische Persönlichkeit*, 1925. Cf. also *MLN*, 34: 371; P. E. More, *The Drift of Romanticism*, 1913. In his short essay *The Turning-Point of My Life*, Mark Twain says that he regarded literature as the most important factor in his life. That this meant "devotion to literature" in both a receiving and a giving sense, there can be little doubt. A lengthy novel like *A Connecticut Yankee at the Court of King Arthur*, which was the result of continuous study of Malory's *Morte D'Arthure* — for which Mark Twain's partiality is well known — and of Walter Scott's novels, which he knew as closely, cannot be explained only as a desire to pour ridicule on Sir Walter. There is an independent inclination for serious literary work behind it all which we would not have suspected if Mark Twain had only been the author of *The Jumping Frog* and innumerable similar pieces. In addition, the above novel is not isolated; we can adduce *The Prince and the Pauper*, *The Gilded Age*, and other works as well. This does not imply that Mark Twain was the hero his biographer Paine wishes to make of him when he says that he was the greatest humorist of all times, the greatest author of world-literature in the 19th century, the greatest American philosopher of his time — all this in spite of his being born in a hovel, like Shakespeare and Jesus Christ (the parallel is Paine's!). It only means that Mark Twain was in reality that sensitive and spiritually cultured man we know from his letters to his wife, as well as from such literary work as *Joan of Arc*. When he says in a letter to a Scotch friend only four years after his marriage that his wife had done wonders with his personality in the course of those years, he is of course speaking in earnest. In calling himself a wild common fellow before she began his education, he goes a bit too far, but the truth glimpses through behind it all. His letter to his wife of Nov. 27th, 1875, definitely reveals a man of refined mind. Cf. *Letters*, pp. 215, 268.

21. Cf. O. H. Moore, *Mark Twain and Don Quixote*, *PMLA*, 37, 324 f.: "... an almost universal prejudice. The popular notion is that Mark Twain's genius 'just grew,' like Topsy; that he was peculiarly a 'self-made' man, the term 'self-made' being understood to mean 'lack in book-learning' ... It will therefore come as a rude shock to many readers ... to know that their favorite drew much of his inspiration for his most American books from European models." Cf. also *A*, 1941, p. 213.

22. "... the Pyramid of Cheops. I could conjure up no comparison that would convey to my mind a satisfactory comprehension of the magnitude of a pile of monstrous stones that covered thirteen acres of ground

and stretched upward four hundred and eighty tiresome feet, and so I gave it up and walked down to the Sphynx. After years of waiting, it was before me at last. The great face was so sad, so earnest, so longing, so patient . . . I shall not speak of the railway for it is like any other railway . . . I shall only say that the fuel they use for the locomotives is composed of mummies 3000 years old, purchased by the ton or by the graveyard for that purpose, and that sometimes one hears the profane engineer call out pettishly: "Damn these plebeians they don't burn worth a cent . . . pass out a King." *New Pilgrims Progress*, pp. 238—40.

23. See *e.g.* O. H. Moore, *Op. cit.*, and Schönemann, *Mark Twain als literarische Persönlichkeit*, 1925.

24. *The Innocents at Home*, p. 43 ff. R. On the strength of new material and practically starting from M. M. Brashear's book on Mark Twain (Univ. N. Carolina, 1934), Ivan Benson has arrived at the result that the author's "western years" were crucial for his development as a literary man. *Mark Twain's Western Years* (Stanford, 1938) is a very painstaking work, correcting a number of mistakes and establishing a firmer chronology of Mark Twain's early writings. Though the scholar stresses the same facts as I, viz. that the early sixties were a turning-point in Mark Twain's literary career, his book is of less importance for my purposes. Professor Benson hardly enters into the necessary literary analysis but investigates mainly — very thoroughly — all exterior circumstances of Mark Twain's early life and material activity, between 1861—66. His attempts to reduce or deny Artemus Ward's and Bret Harte's influence — an influence which Mark Twain himself stressed — fail to convince me. That the incidental condemnation of Bret Harte's character or the latter's failure to publish some of Mark Twain's stories, should impair the value of the literary schooling acknowledged by Mark Twain, does not seem probable to me. Professor Benson's bibliography, pp. 167—174, is very valuable, likewise his Appendix with texts, pp. 175—213.

25. Cf. *e. g.* A. Killen, *Le roman terrifiant*, 1924.

26. *Ib.*, p. 49. Though there can be no doubt about Mark Twain's intention of here attacking the terror novel, it might be pointed out that, about this very time, he began an elaborate parody of the "roman noir." It was called *Awful Terrible Medieval Romance* and it got as far as a fifth chapter. The essence of it was that a German nobleman's only daughter was forced by her father to grow up in the disguise of a son, a fact which implied terrible complications. The little skit has some additional lines in R (*The Jumping Frog* etc., p. 192 ff.). According to a note in the *Author's National Edition*, it was written about 1868. The appended note in R seems to imply that Mark Twain intended a thrust at *Harper's* for still indulging in terror novels. We have no proofs to support the hypothesis that the German setting of this parody should refer to Cooper's two novels with a German (Swiss) background, — on the lines of the terror novel and Scott — viz. *The Heidenmauer* and *The Headsman*.

27. Cf. *e. g.* C. W. Storck, *The Influence of the Popular Ballad on Wordsworth and Coleridge*, PMLA, XXIX, pp. 299 ff.

28. Cf. O. Elton, *A Survey of English Literature 1780—1830*. I, pp. 300 f., 447 f; C. O. Parsons, *Scott's Translation of Bürger's Das Lied von Treue*, JEGPh, 1934, pp. 240 ff.; M. C. Boatwright, *Scott's Theory and Practice Concerning the Use of the Supernatural in Prose Fiction*, PMLA, 1935, pp. 235 ff.

29. Cf. also B. R. Mc Elderry, *Coleridge's Revision of The Ancient Mariner*, StPh, 1932, pp. 68 ff.

30. Cf. *e. g.* RLC, 1928. p. 193.

31. *Poetical Works* (Oxford Poets), p. 48 f.

58 S. B. LILJEGREN

32. In *The Innocents at Home*, the author says that "the vehicle that bears *The Aged Pilot Man* was probably suggested by the old song called "The Raging Canal," but I cannot remember now. The chief idea came from elsewhere" (p. 50 f., R).

33. *The Innocents at Home*, pp. 50 ff. R.

34. Cf. O. Elton, *A Survey of English Literature 1730—1780*, II, p. 67: "The Elegy, from the first, has been profusely imitated, parodied, and translated into ancient and modern languages." Cf. *ib.*, pp. 307 ff.; R. A. Aubin, *Three Notes on "Graveyard" Poetry, PMLA*, 1935, pp. 103 ff. Also P. Van Tieghem, *La poésie de la nuit et des tombeaux en Europe au XVIIIe siècle*, 1921; cf. *RLC*, 1927, pp. 667 ff.; R. Michéa, *Le "plaisir des tombeaux" au XVIIIe siècle, RLC*, 1938, pp. 87 ff.; G. Roth, *Lamartine et le cimetière de campagne de Th. Gray, RLC*, 1923, pp. 651 ff.

35. Th. Moore, *Poetical Works* (Oxford Poets), p. 236.

36. Th. Hood, *Poetical Works* (Oxford Poets), p. 346.

37. *Information Wanted and Other Sketches* (R), p. 11. Cf. also R. A. Aubin, *Op. cit.*

38. *Poetical Works* (Oxford Poets), p. 236 ff. Cf. also *Op. cit.*, p. 254: *On the Detraction Which Followed the Publication of a Certain Poem.*

39. Byron, *Englisch Bards*, 245 f.

40 For the history of *Peter Bell*, see *A*, 47, pp. 136 ff.

Wordsworth's ballad attained particular notoriety on account of the following circumstances: *Peter Bell* was held back for more than twenty years, being written in the spring of 1798 and published only in 1819. Its existence in MS was known for a long time and so it was necessarily much talked of *before* publication. A now forgotten poet, J. H. Reynolds, profited from Wordworth's delay and brought out a parody on his ballad style *in general*, some weeks before the actual appearance of the real *Peter Bell*. This parody was also called *Peter Bell*, which explains the fact that Shelley called *his* parody (written in Oct., 1819, but published only in 1839) *Peter Bell the Third*, Reynolds parody being termed "antenatal" by Shelley.

This "antenatal" *Peter Bell* was very witty and aroused wild enthusiasm in literary circles where Wordsworth's "hypertrophie du moi," his platitudes, his misplaced naturalism, his tearfulness, and his silly repetitions had long been held in contempt. Its content might be summed up like this: A half-witted old man, Peter Bell, is walking by moonlight in a churchyard. After discovering a tombstone indicating William Wordsworth's grave, his tears dry up, and he walks home smiling, feeling very happy that W. W. will not write poems about him any more. The 42 stanzas are full of allusions to those of Wordsworth's poems which were regarded as most inane, like *Lucy Gray, The Idiot Boy, The Leech-Gatherers, The Pet-Lamb*, and others:

> " . . . .
> He hath a noticeable look,
> This old man hath — this grey old man;
> . . . . .
> 'Tis Peter Bell — 'tis Peter Bell,
> . . . . .
> In winter he is very cold.
> I've seen him in the month of August,
> At the wheat-field, hour by hour,
> Picking ear, — by ear, — by ear, —
> Through the wind, — and rain, — and sun, — and shower,
> From year, — to year, — to year, — to year.
> . . . . .
> Betty Foy — *My* Betty Foy,
> Is the aunt of Peter Bell;

. . . . .
He is rurally related;

. . . . .
But Peter Bell he hath no brother.
Not a brother owneth he,
Peter Bell he hath no brother;
His mother had no other son,
No other son e'er called her mother;
Peter Bell hath brother none.

. . . . .
Peter Bell is laughing now,
Like a dead man making faces;
Never saw I smile so old,
On face so wrinkled and so cold,
Since the Idiot Boy's grimaces.

. . . . .
He is stooping now about
O'er the grave-stones one and two;

. . . . .
The Ancient Marinere lieth here,
Never to rise, although he pray'd

. . . . .
He reads — "Here lieth W. W.
Who will never more trouble you, trouble you."

. . . . .
He quits that moon-light yard of skulls,
And still he feels right glad, and smiles
With moral joy at that old tomb;
Peter's cheek recalls its bloom.
And as he creepeth by the tiles,
He mutters ever — "W. W.
Never more will trouble you, trouble you."
Here endeth the ballad of Peter Bell."

More parodies and burlesque notes and reviews followed in quick succession, till literary circles buzzed with them and one of the most memorable scandals of English Romanticism had been instigated. Among such parodies, *The Dead Asses* was out within a couple of months, continuing the vein of ridicule launched by Reynolds even if he was not the author. Byron took up the matter in the 3rd canto of *Don Juan* and in the following year he wrote an epilogue to Wordsworth's ballad which is very scathing:

"There's something in stupid ass,
And something in a heavy dunce;
But never since I went to school
I heard or saw so damned a fool
As William Wordsworth is for once;
I really wish that Peter Bell
And he who wrote it were in hell,
For writing nonsense for the nonce." Etc.

It is evident that the publication of *Peter Bell* was one of the most sensational events in English Romanticism, and it was never forgotten. As late as 1839, Mrs Shelley thought it worth while to publish Shelley's parody.

41. *The Stolen White Elephant* (Everett), p. 106 ff.
42. *Life on the Mississippi*, II, p. 62 f. (T).

43. *Ib.*, p. 98 f. (T).
44. *Ib.*, p. 100 (T).
45. *Ib.*, p. 100 (T).
46. *Ib.*, p. 103 f. (T).
47. *Ib.*, p. p. 105 ff. (T).
48. See *PMLA*, 37, 324 f.
49. *Fingal*, I.
50. *Temora*, VI.
51. *Berrathon*.
52. Cf. M. H. Miller, *Chateaubriand and English Literature*, 1925, Ch. III.
53. Cooper's break with *literary* tradition as regards the picture of the Indian presented in earlier literature is very obvious. Cf. *e. g.* M. B. Bissell, *The American Indian in English Literature of the 18th Century* (Yale Studies in English), 1925.

That the language of Cooper's Indians was a poetic creation and not the real thing, was pointed out at once by the critics of *The Last of the Mohicans*. Some of the critics were very harsh with the author, but none seems to have found out his source, *viz. Ossian*:

"In *The Last of the Mohicans*, and in *The Prairie*, scarcely a conversation can be found in which questions are directly asked and directly answered. We quote... 'He gave them tongues, like the false call of the wild cat; hearts like rabbits; the cunning of the hog (but none of the fox) and arms longer than the legs of the moose... 'This is not the manner in which Indians talk, nor is it the manner in which any people talk."

The North American Review, April 1828, p. 374.

". . . about as much like the speech of a true Indian orator as a bad imitation of bad poetry would be like the speech of a man of business . . ." *Godey's Lady's Book*, p. 267, quoted in M. Clavel, *Fenimore Cooper*, 1938, p. 604, note.

Perhaps Parkman's criticism ought to carry most weight, as his knowledge of Indian history and manners was unrivalled. Of *The Last of the Mohicans*, he says: "We do not allude to his Indian characters, which it must be granted, are for the most part either superficially or falsely drawn; while the long conversations which he puts into their mouths are as truthless as they are tiresome." Quoted in M. Clavel, *Fenimore Cooper and his Critics*, 1938, p. 322.

54. *Deerslayer*, Ch. XIV.
55. *Ib.*, Ch. IX.
56. *Ib.*, Ch. XV.
57. *The Last of the Mohicans*, Ch. XXIX.
58. *Ib.*, Ch. XXX.
59. *Ib.*, Ch. XXXIII.
60. *A Visit to Niagara* (in *Information Wanted* R), p. 17 ff.
61. *A Yankee at the Court of King Arthur*, II (T), p. 252 ff. Whether Mark Twain here intended to strike also at Cooper's medieval novels *(The Heidenmauer)*, is uncertain.
62. *My First Literary Adventure*, p. 111 *(Author's National Edition)*.

S. B. LILJEGREN.